The Uncertainty Principle
Poems at 70

The Uncertainty Principle
Poems at 70

by

Richard Stuecker

Cover design by Shay Culligan

ISBN: 978-1-952326-37-0

Kelsay Books
502 South 1040 East, A-119
American Fork, Utah, 84003

Acknowledgments

A number of journals have been kind enough to publish poems included in this chapbook. These include:

Cabrillo Quarterly: "Espresso 2"

Former People Journal: "Assumption Day," "The Uncertainty Principle"

Main Street Rag: "At Last Snow," "Espresso 1"

Pegasus: early versions of "Equinox," "Madame and the Bones," "Askew"

Red Coyote: "Espresso 4"

Poetica: "Evening Walk"

Stillwater Review: "Spring Weeding"

Tilde: "My Grandfather's Binoculars"

Tipton Poetry Review: "Slippage"

In Appreciation

I want to thank the staff of the Bluegrass Writers Studio, whose classes and workshops have enabled me to write at a level where my work is being accepted by literary journals. I especially want to thank my program director, Robert D. Johnson, Julie Hensley, Carter Sickles, Nancy Jensen, Christina Lovin, and Young Smith. They have inspired me with their own works and their critiques and responses to my work. Thanks to BGWS graduate and Associate Professor B. J. Wilson, who has been a constant writing companion and editor. Finally, thanks to my wife, Barbara, for her support and patience.

Contents

When it comes, it cannot be checked;
When it goes, it cannot be stopped.
—Lu Chi

My Grandfather's Binoculars

At sunrise at Scituate,
the North Atlantic coast
begins to warm itself from winter.
I sit by the ancient lighthouse
at Cedar Point with my grandfather's binoculars
watching the sailing school of fledgling sailors
hoist their sheets against the easterly breeze,
two-man catboats following a schooner,
setting out of the harbor to Nantucket Sound
in their yellow bucket hats anxious
for a day of freedom on the restful ocean.

I came in summer when I was young
every year my grandmother brought me
to this exact bench, handing me
my grandfather's heavy glasses.
I did not know him, my grandfather,
but grandmother pointed out Five Cliffs,
and Peggity Beach, so I would know
where our people came from
when they came across the sea;
so I could recite the stories she told
about them, but never did she tell me
the mystery of my grandfather.

I have come to Scituate haphazardly
since she died, now I am aging.
Still, the schooner and the catboats sail
off to Nantucket and still the gulls
and cormorants squawk, dive for fish,
wrangle for tidbits left by young families
who stay the day along the narrow beach,
the lighthouse having stood another nor'easter.
Still I come to the same bench at dawn,
the sun fattens in a sky flecked with clouds,

I lift his binoculars to my eyes,
knowing this is where he left her
pregnant, with a nameless child.

The Uncertainty Principle

Today I awaken in my own bed,
at first alarmed, then relieved,
in the window across the room
a forsythia bush exploding
yellow buds filling the glass panes.

Yesterday,
I was confined within metal
fall bars, arm punctured with needles,
everything an inch out of reach:
my nurse's call button.
A white brigade, confounded by
a microbe they cannot name,
blocked a vibrant, flaming bouquet,
nervous that over time they cannot
cure my end stage disease.

Later, when I revive enough to drive
I plan to bring my aging mother
brilliant flowers, positioning
them at the center of her window,
blocking her view overlooking
Saint Michael's where crocuses spring forth
randomly about stones and statues
while bursting forsythia and dogwoods
draw the eye skyward, where robins
are nesting in the forks of ash trees.

Spring Weeding

My garden ages me in April
even as it sprouts and early blooms
pop out of the earth I left untended,
lonely, tired and lazy last fall
my father warned me not to over plant
when I was young enough to carry stone,
dig beds, plant perennials, lay mulch.
Who listens to fathers when one is
young enough to pattern flagstone
patios and paths, dig rich soil?
Who remembers when one becomes
the age when one's father died
what he said on his knees pulling weeds
spilling over granite rocks demarking
beds from walkways while his words
uncovered barriers and cracks anew?
His words loving me in so practical
a way, surround me as I whack dandelion clusters,
reveal stone walks. They come back to me
in whispers and exasperation,
knowing his son would plant too much
allowing returning growth to exhaust him
as his own garden, once tilled so precisely,
overwhelmed what his father said to him
while kneeling and weeding together at dusk.

Weed Killer

With vengeance,
salt and vinegar
in my sprayer,
loathing in my heart,
indefatigable,
I take them out,
creeping charley,
robin runaway,
gangly vines roped
around ferns
Stems of daylilies,
running up
trellis and arch,
springing up
in cracks
between rocks,
strangling perennials,
covering walkways
at will.

Using my grandmother's
killer recipe
written in her hand
on the back page of
her practical
dependable cookbook,
I stalk the defenseless
like a mine detector
slaying the living
so beauty might live
at my discretion.

Espresso 1

Espresso in a cup lifted
from the Café Chiado,
rich, bitter, darkness
reminiscent of the deep
pleasure taken engaging
in so many delicious sins
described delicately by
my parish priest's sermons.
Partaking of so many of the fruits,
trees of knowledge, plunging
into sweet, idyllic, oblivion,
identifying bad companions,
near occasions of sin, thank you
Sister Raymounda, for directing me,
instructing me, your guidance
to real life, where I suffer pain,
satisfaction of work. Ecstatic,
profound, enlightening moments,
the final embrace of the Angel of Death.

Espresso 2

Espresso brewed in an
Italian maker traveled
from a bin at the
Mercato di Lucca
in the shade of the wall
surrounding the Centro
poured in small cups
stolen from the Café Chiado
in Lisboa, sipped on my porch
this strangely cool morning in
August when temperatures
ought to be scorching.
Your unexpected call
detailing your new life
break dances my heart.
Bitter caffeine lingers, as does
the remnant of the crushed
beans in the bottom of the cup.
A sparrow dips itself into
a chipped porcelain teapot
I refuse to part with as a
tiny lizard explores aging
brickwork needing tuckpointing,
birdsong surrounds, stirring thoughts,
you finding your way away from me.
The morning warms until
I carry my empty cup inside
to rinse out the dregs.

Espresso 3

Ironic and hypocritical
sipping the best espresso
reading the horrors in the *Times,*
awaiting a friend, while
children at the border await
release from cages,
separated from their mother's breasts,
sipping this bitter brew,
I become aware
how I am dulled by tweets,
sliding into the slough
of my basest self,
willing to justify myself
because the coffee is so damn
devilishly rich and good.

Espresso 4

A dense summer
Cinzano umbrellas'
shadows cast
across wrought iron
lacy tables;
sipping simple
espresso noting
lackadaisical drivers,
stalled at rush hour;
wondering what universe
lies within each driver
what family horror,
what travesty, triumph,
what dull routine,
what plan for later,
yearning; scanning who
in this slanted café
sees me, sees them?

Equinox

At twilight
fish sleep
suspended—
a cut glass bowl
once held
roses against
mid-winter sun;
dust defines
a narrow hall,
shadows slope
down hardwood,
half awake
awaiting,
darkness slips
over the city,
fog creeps
hides stars,
doorways disappear,
misty streets slide,
empty alleys,
a cat yelps
a door slams.
Silence

Madame and the Bones

Madame appears under
tuberous begonias, amuses
scented ladies, shuffles lies,

smiles; a searing sun slants
shadows up white-washed walls,
une divertissement d'ete.

Scattered, slid across slate,
the bones lie, unread,
les destinées de Madame ont jeté.

Forgotten under iron grates—
decayed debris, mingle
spruce, honeysuckle, juniper;

moonlight white, they wait, as
night snakes sliver over moist stone,
disappear to secrets inside the earth.

Courting Memories

Fat sun at mid-summer,
we trek several miles,
walking, jogging, skipping:
boxers up the parkway,
dropping down to composite courts.
Rackets stretch sunward,
phantom serves, forehands,
backhands, overheads,
through sinister air,
serve, backhand, rally
torquing, reaching
a winner down the line.
Shadows lengthen across clay,

Maybe we'll avoid the draft—
Maybe there is a God—
Maybe we'll travel to China—
Maybe we'll see the Stones—
Maybe we'll meet up tomorrow—
Maybe tonight we might get lucky—
Maybe we won't.

Yellow lights stretch across
a church parking lot, thumping drum,
Youth Dew and English Leather
mom-pressed Bermudas, white Izods,
I eye him eying her as
he spins a joke. I recall a story.
Staccato rhythm, stumbling feet—
a formless slow sway sliding
the only dance I can manage,
dream of soft scented body
under translucent Japanese lamps.

Assumption Day

Regret and reminiscence float over dense August
like camel-forming clouds, until a crisp day
silences the season with a killing frost.
Sucking into my lungs molds,
the death of flowering weeds,
my dusty garden droops
untended for weeks beyond
the deck rail where I lounge on a chaise lounge—
weather, cool as the Cape in June,
draws me out for a supermarket croissant,
a cup of Keurig Italian Bold, chill
enough to consider a cigarette, I deny
the pleasure and embrace the caffeine,
tasting a bitter coffee.
Mosquitoes nibbling at my sock tops, I
wonder who sits at my table now in Lisbon
at the Café Chiado, greets Vera, sips espresso
savors savory and sweet as the day ahead might be?

Evening Walk

An urgent wind thrusts us,
relents an occasional pause
to our daily walk. Not knowing
what might blow in,
our faulty pace quickens us
to remember much we lost
that meant everything once,
now flutter, swirl, vanish
into the moonless sky.
Turning back, we always turn
toward where we come from,
against chill reminiscence
rising less and less, more and more
we lock the door to still the night.

Oaks

Walking under shivering oaks,
saplings in the '30s, now giants,
I wonder as they sway
before the storm coming
if they fear for themselves, as lately
they seem to be taken one by one
having so long flexed and swirled
but stood their ground?
Only last October they glorified the fall,
more brilliant than any year in memory.
Now, stark December, only the oaks
resist dropping withered leaves.
Maples, elms, dogwoods, ashes make
barren forms against the snow-filled clouds,
allowing us to track the falcon that moved in
last spring and the waning moon that
hid all summer. This storm may twist
them until they crack or uproot fallen
trunks as tall as I am walking by.
Some kind neighbor has stacked
a log pile of hard woods
outside our back door. I toss
one onto our fire, watch the fire rise,
hold her wise hand in mine.
A furious roar settles to glow.

At Last, Snow

At last, snow—
in a Mohave of a winter.
Thank God for warm weather—some say;
I prefer snow or
I would move to Scottsdale, eat
Scarsdale salads in the dry desert;
rub tinctures into withered skin
deal another hand of hearts,
bid slowly as my body decays.

I have been wistful for snow,
layering side streets and gardens
like my mother layered
buttercream on cooling jam cakes.
The promise of no school.
The joy of hurling my body at breakneck speed
on my father's rickety American Flyer
unbound by gravity and consent.

Slippage

Much of what was
seems to slip like warmth
over the jam under the door
through the cracked window
we never look through
in the closet we leave
wearing new clothes.
I want to say to her:
That wasn't it,
it wasn't like that at all
no, not at all. Even
though you have the facts
like a game show contestant
or an entry in Wikipedia
or a poem filled with
clever lines that loses
its nuance in the cadence.
Even if I were to stuff
the jam with rags and
newsprint from yesterday
or glazed the forgotten window
still the sadness and emptiness
would stay while vivacity
through a mousehole would
find its way to slip out and away.

Scoundrel Time

Our house prepared for imminent invasion,
family, friends, strangers might
penetrate our battlements,
slide inward through some
forgotten priest hole,
purloin our treasury,
carry secrets to secrets
in the moon-free night.

How vulnerable the coffin klatch?
What lies within the basket
you carry into my kitchen?
Arcane knowledge disguised as truth?
Something once read surfing the net?
A growing list of names?

Well, everyone knows how he is,
his dusty garden cultivating weeds,
his house needs painting and who knows
how many guns fill his basement arsenal?

We chat outside the coffee house.
Inside the writers type Kafka;
I drink a latte, you an herbal tea.
A drunk accosts us, we offer help,
he staggers off, heading nowhere
along the wide street cars clog their way,
to ends and means and matters and musings.

Askew

The Pole Star, it seems,
is a few degrees askew
true north bends truth,
curves upward, away—
moss is not to be trusted—
and I wonder in this
season of turnings
which turning veers which way?

I search for a still point
find only the fitful
dancing of dogs to exhaustion—
the yelp of new beginnings
turning to ends—no end in sight—
a garden full of expectations
bursts forth out of hollow earth.

Patterson

How many brilliant poems
have I lost in the early dawn
too lazy to reach for my notebook
curled up cozy against my wife, or
more likely, reached for my pen,
only to discover awakening to
nonsense and banality scrawled
on my notebook pages that
seemed such genius at 2 AM?
A poem-hungry bulldog waits
expectant to chew my verses and
lap them up with its literary tongue.

Chant

How is it we long for something
we think we want or haven't a clue,
following frayed flags and kites
over bridges to infernos
we think will fill an emptiness
found just around the corner
where we will meet someone
or find something we lost some time
ago or missed receiving from those
who should have known better?
How is it we make people
into other people who were not there
to begin with or were inept or
too busy seeking something
they failed to receive, so
I make you into the parent
I wanted or the child I neglected
or the sibling who moved quickly
to a corner of the world seeking
what he or she couldn't find or
wanted to escape, seeking by the sea,
hiking up a climb or staying back,
taking care of someone
instead of our own longing?
Can it be true that what we long for
can be found eating mushrooms,
chanting with a multitude
seeking climax we might have once
felt or thought we did, or did?
Is the illusion of giving to others only
giving to ourselves?

How is it we feel an ecstasy we project
on some natural grandeur that has no meaning
except the meaning we paint or write or sing;
trek to some apparition, some being
said to be a godhead, seeking

in the Mother's embrace instant salving
waiting in a line of penitents to receive
darshan, the blessing promised, the vision?
Promising ourselves we will not be the same,
we seek to love with a purity others, ourselves;
aging, looking back on what we
might have done, been or given do we
seek forgiveness or simply become pilgrims
Lourdes, Ladakh, Camino de Santiago or
perhaps to a desk in a quiet place to seek
the making of a nearly perfect poem?

Chartres

Longing for pilgrimage:
the quiet and simple, even
among the throngs; I am
unfit to walk the Camino Santiago,
it does not draw me
as does Notre Dame de Chartres,
the Madonna in her celestial space
built of stone and story in the windows.

Longing to surrender to clarity,
to empty my vessel, fill my void
with completeness gained by
falling deep into the abyss of love,
endless embrace, no expectation or
understanding, seeking the eternal
connection your builders sought
constructing your earthly home.

Longing to enter into the sacred blue light,
believe like common artisans
within the stone silence buttressed
by faith, walk the labyrinth
to the center of transformation
not to perfection, to be comforted,
my heart touched by the warmth of grace,
the Mother's kiss soothing my lost self.

About the Author

Richard Stuecker is a poet and writer who graduated from Duke University in 1970. A Pushcart Prize nominee, he is a graduate of the Bluegrass Writer's Studio MFA program at Eastern Kentucky University. His poems have appeared in or been accepted by *Tilde, Former People, Pegasus, Main Street Rag, Poetica and District Lit;* creative nonfiction in *Fleas on the Dog, Hippocampus, Connotation Press, Brilliant Flash Fiction, Crambo, Louisville Magazine,* and *Delmarva Review;* book reviews in the Louisville *Courier-Journal.* A collection of essays on conscious aging, *Vibrant Emeritus,* was published in 2014 by John Hunt Publishing (London). Ric lives in Louisville, Kentucky, with his wife of 47 years, where he dotes on his four grandchildren: Marley, Sylvia, Lucy, and Dane.